D1525693

THIS WAY OUT

THIS WAY OUT
by Carmine Starnino

For Debra,

Best wishes

On (I hope)

a great career.

Carmine Starnino

London 2012

GASPEREAU PRESS
PRINTERS & PUBLISHERS
2009

For Jen & Lucca

NEXT DOOR CAFÉ

We were bored, so we stayed. The days knocked deep
into other days. A glacialness set in, and life kept pace
with the dried fruit in the jar. Brushed steel gave back
our pissed-off bits, our doubled selves so drained of disguise
we forgot where it was we were hoping to go, holed up
all summer in a corner so dark you'd half expect bison
chalked on a cave-face every time we cadged a light.
It was the kind of place where morning fell for everyone
but harder for some, where bad decisions were lived
counter-clockwise, and endlessly refitted to finish up flush,
where afternoons were a gradual squander of sobriety,
shot glasses lamped with whisky on cue and empties
were the crags of a quandary drunkenness clung to.
Tables where, outside the shrieking reach of the talkers,
can't-sleeps stayed and night-shifters cooled their heels
attended by soul-tools: cellphone, lighter, cigarette.
Nights of middle-aged men enduring middle-aged men
in their cups, buying rounds, half-cusped on high stools.
Sun-up found a few run aground, upshouldered hulls,
while our own lives were an endless keel-scrape where
the pluperfect errand was the errand always deferred.
A kind of time travel, I guess. We sat back and watched
the future screen its clichés of us: those besuited
and briefcased, with their died-and-gone-to-heaven whistle
when handed a pint; those done-to-a-turn divorcees
in duffle coat and boots (wine-sipping casualties of the wife wars);
those who, smashed, stand too suddenly slewing into you,
and those who, if you join, you join uninvited.

OUR BUTCHER

I could bone up, be the right man for that one-man job,
hang by its hocks a rabbit shucked from the jacket
of its black-bristled fur and still talking in twitches.
As well, I might grasp the particular way he swings

a cleaver, brings it down on a neck like a primitive.
More to the point, I'd learn to move the beak of my blade
into the fragrance of a flank, or browse apart a chest's
cardiac leafage, my white apron a blotchwork of blood.

I'd like to pickle ox tongue and pig feet, screw lids
on sheep tripe and calf brain, set out jars like indices
to carcasses unpacked like suitcases. Striated and plush,
crewelworked with fat and grosgrained with gristle,

meat is not semblance, meat is baroque. That said,
I'd love to break back the pages of a shank and read all day.
Tales about the flex and kick, the squawk and gack
of things in pens: grass-nipping goats, had-been hens,

hogs which nuzzled mud and snorkelled its odours
until their plug was pulled and the spinning gears
stilled to small organs, organs I'd like to disinter and wrap,
risen again inside the pink of new paper skin.

FRONT DOOR

Hard knock past,
  weather eye open,
streetwise. Light-headed
  swung wide,
feeling the floor fall away,
  but holds fast,
a fistful of slamming
  in whose shadow
we've put down our lives.
  The way out, in plain sight.
High C squeak
  the soundtrack
with which we pull it shut and go,
  thumb thumbing
a lift to the jamb,
  and how, bolting for work,
you (yes, you)
  always let it just hang there,
aching in a decimal of space
  that waits for me
to get the fuck up,
  round things off
firmly. Stands its ground,
  choosing territory
over travel. No two ways,
  no questions asked.
One ear cocked
  for footstep, heel of hand, key.
Back late, we find it
  asleep on its feet.

VITA BREVIS

Short back and long bangs, but our barber never got it right.
Gentile's place—you know it. Two leather chairs, mirror,
clipper, newspaper, radio on low, everything lit in one hue.
I'd bring my GQ photo. *What the hell kind of hairstyle is that?*
Self-knowledge was always knowledge of what I was not.
In my native buzz-cut, I bummed around Chabanel's neo-realist lots.
Its loading docks and sweatshop façades true dead ringers
for their film-set selves, later made famous by my handheld shot
of factory women running in rain to catch the 121 after work.
Such perfectly cast amateurs: transparently simple, scarcely acting.
Born there, but never local enough to play the part,
I tried to look busy in that open-air theatre of storm clouds and asphalt.
We all did. We danced to soundtracks taped off CHOM.
Chose "Beh" over the thee and thou of "I see your point."
Studied the sitcoms, plagiarists of inner-city high-fives.
Even our doors were class-conscious: fake-grained, pretend-cut
from the knot of some oak. Critics called us an intelligent contribution
to the working-class genre, a landmark of contrapuntal clichés:
the southerly effect of washing on lines, tomato gardens;
the northerly effect of strip clubs, warehouses, high-rises.
A stomping ground that never lost the feel of being the place
where bad weather always chewed up our shooting time,
where Québécois girls were eager body doubles for the nice daughters
we later married, where alleyways obliged our alter egos
to make good their escape, our mothers calling.
I put in long hours shadowing myself as I walked the tracks,
stopping to let the trains go by—always a five-minute
footage of freight cars, each one empty. I wanted the real thing

at work in real time for that foredefeated mood—artistically crude, yes,
but how much more genuine! Cut to the angry young man
shouting taunts from the overpass. Early Truffaut chasing
late Rossellini. I once found a watch still ticking, and left it.

SHAG

Nearly put me off sleep for good, so high,
distressed and unrelenting was the sound.
But then, isn't that the point, that it begged
to be heard? Across the alley, behind a fence
with around-the-clock junk, an animal
pled its case: nicotine-yellow, upthrust rump,
heart-shaped face trapped in a bestial, blunt,
eyes-shut rendition of lust. Like the first
salt taste of a woman: the scream of my body
hormonally deranged. Unspayed, unsated,
singing its song of woe, of whoa, an *a cappella*
punk yodel that dogged me back to bed.

HEAVENOGRAPHY

Working-class clouds are up to speed. All day, they blow apart. All day, they bloom back: churning, thick-piled, and already beginning to fray. Working-class clouds are swept from somewhere else to right here. Working-class clouds are stuck in traffic, idling, inching ahead. Working-class clouds are old pros at the god-like point of view, gaze down at the backs of birds in flight, at pinhead people. Working-class clouds sit tight and bull's-eye every new space they hit. Working-class clouds tiptoe neck and neck, pitter pat, at good clip, understudying each other, taking a stab at lookalikeness, becoming clones, or close enough. Working-class clouds eke out their melt, morph on the installment plan, think-twice fleet, vite, and then some. Working-class clouds dig deep, 3pm and still clocking klicks, legging it longwise. Working-class clouds make tracks over the working-class. Working-class clouds take turns taking down directions, try to read back what they wrote, but can't. Working-class clouds are tripping, sensing just how high up they are. Working-class clouds are a thousand tons of rereturned rain freshly painted and set upright to dry. Working-class clouds are breeze-fed flocs, hardly anything, whathaveyous, an idea in trial and error, one-of-a-kind demos. Working-class clouds are self-made men, having brung themselves up from street level, from scratch. Working-class clouds could give a shit, represent nothing more than atmospheric farting around, a bunch of good-for-nothings stuck between going and gone. Working-class clouds hold the air in white hands, like babies at suck. Working-class clouds bob this way and that. Working-class clouds touch down safely in the higher precipices, leave appreciable skid marks. Working-class clouds are built in a hurry from random parts: scraps of billow, lengths of bulge. Working-class clouds are beamed in live, a real-time film of floating, sky broadcasting endless eyewitness accounts of itself. Working-class clouds, deadline looming, knuckle under, get to grips with the situation, mutter *here goes* and go hard at it. Working-class clouds are above it all, regard the hydraulics that give them their height as a right. Working-class clouds don't really know who's running the show. Working-class clouds are what happens when sky works up a full head of steam with nowhere to go. Working-class clouds are uploaded fluorescence, exoskeletal shingles of light, bits of 2-D happenstance our eye is always on. Working-class clouds are the dribs and drabs of a slow leak: *pffft*. Working-class clouds are flat tires slapping the road for mile-on-mile. Working-class clouds are taking on water and soon will singlemindedly bail. Working-class clouds live large, late-Turner doozies that fit flank to flank, close ranks, press-ganged and darkening. For working-class clouds, ill winds are a real buzz kill. Working-class clouds always run out of time, and when that happens we catch the wetness full in the face and sprint from street to park shelter and wait. Working-class clouds, your head in them.

THIS WAY OUT

Corkscrew staircases, triplexes, satellite
dishes. Such riches as oranges—buck-fifty
a pound—piled on slats, under awnings,
and south of rue Ogilvy's stretch
of family-run sweet-shops and delis:
Pêcherie Mairmais, where, head to tail,
cod cool on crushed ice. A good price.

It suits me down to the ground, this place
of sodium-lit nowhereness between
Jean-Talon and St. Roch. Its eighteen-
nineteenths of a toehold on the world.
Flattops beside flattops, planted
in acres of concrete—ungentrified
Eden at the brink of the sticks: Parc Ex,

God said, and up sprang sidestreets of shoebox
flats (plus rats), chain-link fences, plain-
penny bricks, and paint-splashed garages.
After that, rust-odoured alleys
where balding towels and pink panties
drip dry together like arranged marriages.
Then Bengali protest posters

and weekend cricket until rain stops play.
Next day, the big-watt rap of double-
parked cars, subfusc bars, sari-clad girls
playing hula hoop, and $2+2=5$
sprayed in red by some effin'
idiot on the hoof. By week's end,
God called forth empty produce boxes

stacked outside *Marché* SPG,
and me dashing out to *Steve's*, low on milk.
God saw it was good: our fourth floor
bolt-hole with a crow's-nest view,
cigarette reek rising from below,
my paper heisted every morning,
and *muezzin* calls from speakers

next door. There's more: the beslippered
Greek men in wife-beaters
like off-broadway Brandos, the Syrian
barbershop brothers in all-weather
flipflops, the *Dollarama* shopping sprees
paid out in small change, the leaves
that rallied into piles and fought

the wind to a standstill, the spice smells,
the tea-coloured strays, the take-home Bombay,
and the half-chugged bottles of plonk
and beer I saw clear an open window.
De Liège in the morning splodged
with crash landings, brown interbled
with the dregs of lives close-quartered

in this burg, this case study in eyesores,
this last word in slumlords, this warren
of walk-ups where the wallpaper's
forever airing out its smell. Hell
or fresh start: a room, a roof, a wage.
And everyone too tired to hold out
for better. The price paid for a new story

of creation: tatted up Sikhs,
bicycling knife-sharpeners, and Bollywood actors,
just off the boat. We are counted
one by one into this dead end,
where the bandwidth's slow and we speak
not speech but yeses and nos that add up
to a scoop of that, a pound of this. What bliss.

NINE FROM ROME

Dear Michael,

Happiness could do worse than our bedsheet's
two-day spell head down outside the window.
Festive with polka-dots, it flaps the span of frame,
catches the sun full on. That, and the damp
in the air makes me think of travel by sea.
Here dryness is something we miss by moments,
the electric heater making a poor fist of it.
T-shirts exude their drip like water clocks,
and the detergent's mouth-to-mouth with the early hour
turns our underwear pheromonal,
filling the room with the scent of aroused communication.
If, as Nietzsche said, we should try to live
always in expectation of some impossible grace,
well, one couldn't do better than this place.

Dear Norm,

Nights we duck in and out of shoe shops
on Via del Corso, because by then I've had enough,
and tired of antiquities, join the droves
alive and giddy for goods that fill the hand,
following in the footsteps of all those who chased the latest thing
and died, leaving relics rescued from time
as we won't be, but hurry to meet it, our sensual self,
to call down its double from a sleek shelf:
low-slung, square-front, suede mule, loafer.
Something extraordinary is always on offer,
and afterwards Jen and I heel it home with items
that redeem us by their price, their fit. And that's just
a start! Five senses tingling from self-ogling,
vanities fresh in bud, we crave a thrill too quick for art.

Dear Eric,

First day we scrape the dogshit from our shoes.
Second finds us on the losing end of the jargon.
Third a storm falls on the city, and the sacking continues
until the fourth when we find ourselves trusting
this routine. Exhaust, graffiti and trash urge us to go,
to do. From our window, the suburb of balconies,
level above level, spreads to uncharted points.
Sunned rooftops nod in their heights. We agree
we don't want to die, but want our souls
to harden into posters peeling from the walls.
The next few days we ride the tram home on its last run
alongside kids back from clubbing, still wired,
still smelling of pot. Mopeds speed us off to sleep
scattering our heartbeats—spondee of rev and roar.

Dear Marius,

Honestly? This rubble-gawking feels like duty,
and ancient history an abstraction sleeping off
its particulars. I like food markets better: awnings
with their two cultures, sun and shade; grocers
who give fresh evidence for everything; the daily bustle;
the chattering buyers of fruit and vegetable.
We might be peasants, field slaves, slum dwellers
dawdling in the breathe-me-deeply air of bread smells,
quickening to the craving incitement of sights
too minor for epics: crammed up boxes of goodly cantaloupes;
tomatoes, whose red day is going well.
We might be ghosts back for the chestnuts' oxblood smoulder,
clementines deleted from tree, twig and leaf intact,
apples greedily lapping greenness from each other.

Dear Robyn,

When we bike past the aqueduct on the Campagna,
arches striding, then abruptly, field, I say good,
let it stop, let our days here be an argument
for a bite to eat, a change of scene, let us join tourists
timelessly milling and churning in the streets
like extras talent-spotted for the stardom of statistics,
let us wallow in the wasteful happiness of travel mispent,
the rich disappointment of the mood itself.
How else catch our insignificance on the wing and outwit it?
We half-watch our whereabouts, the newness
of remnants we've no name for, something-somethings that whisk past,
once seen and never forgotten. The guidebooks
beckon with you-are-here facts. The guidebooks can wait.
We've got a table at Da Gino, and we're running late.

Dear David,

I wake in the small hours with big thoughts.
Mortality, mostly. How arches, pillars, colonnades
drive the message home: a civilization gone for good
and buried beneath. But even extinction can be done to death.
You're next, jaws of wall hiss at me. I shrug.
Ruins are a great place to catch your breath after shopping.
Sundays we roam Porta Portese's all-direction
sprawl of stalls; fast-taking merchants, quick as get.
Here oblivion is driven out by cheap editions
and good knock-offs, lo-fi gewgaws and ziggurats of baubles,
down at hem skirts and misdemeanoured hats,
ribbon-tied letters complete with old bureau.
Centuries are turned on like a tap, then caught in dusty bottles,
ink-dark, shelved beside potted cuttings two for a euro.

Dear Geoff,

9:00 pm, and our usual walk to Trastevere.
Up Quarto Venti, left on Gianicolense,
until two roads diverge, and we take neither,
descend, instead, the uriney gloom of stone steps,
spirited into throng-loudness, well-litness,
gelato queues, vendors selling glowsticks,
and carnival acts. We take our place among
couples circulating among pagan shades,
until we're ready to deal ourselves back in,
ascend the high-sided rock, re-enter our level,
traffic lights clicking through their signals
with only the two of us there, in that hereafter
of pastel-drab apartments piled on our hill.
Then home: my desk-lamp, her sleep-silence.

Dear Asa,

Picture us: hand in hand along cobbled streets
that drink the dusk neat, thousand-year-old cul-de-sacs
and the smell of bosk. Distance has been folded and put away.
Views are something to walk toward until we get there.
But let's be frank. That Jen and I have fetched up
in this city of pilgrims, sightseers and supplicants
—gone from were to we're, you might say—
can't hide the fact I'm on the run. Tired of the crossroad
where push comes to shove (the bad poems X writes,
the stupid reviews Y pens), I've snuck off,
a flit to a sunny flat, out of touch, much taken
with this and that, with such and such. No rush
as I take in life through my mouth, sip cappuccino.
Call my truce with the world: Pax Starnino.

Dear Mary,

What I believe in now are doldrum days,
days of kicking back on one of Christendom's rooftops,
the self getting a good whiff of its sloth.
A skyline, half-hazed, of aerials and satellite dishes
gratifies me, a clock-free, in situ serenity
born from harder days, which aren't these days,
these are days of no forwarding address and no one to meet,
days of bearings not taken and heels dug in,
days of unpoemed emotions I'm too tranquil to recollect—
days off, in other words, less said, more meant,
small talk undressed down to Hmm or Meh.
Time to kill, I watch an odd-job man in overalls
prime a wall white, alfresco. Truly, the veriest words
are like watercolours conveyed onto plaster, which may fade.

PUGNAX GIVES NOTICE

He's done with it, the tridents and tigers,
the manager's greed, the sumptuous beds
of noble women who please their own moods.
He's done with dogging it for the crowds,
the stabbing, the slashing, the strangling,
the poor pay, the chintzy palm branch prizes.
Make no mistake. Pugnax is a real fierceosaurus.
Winner of 26 matches, a forum favourite.
Yet his yob genes have, it seems, gone quiet.
Fatigue has called his soul back to his body.
Circles under his eyes; he sleeps badly.
Late-night cigs lit from the dog-end of the last,
cutwork of the clock nibbling him small.
In the barracks around him his friends snore,
lucky returnees of the last hard hacking,
dead to the world, free of a weapon in the fist.
Priscus face-down in the crook of his arm.
Triumphus flung open, caught on a bad turn.
Verus collapsed, whacked, against the cot.
Flamma, doomed by down-thumbing shadows,
lies in a stain of his final shape and size.
Pugnax loves them all, chasers and net-fighters,
fish-men and javelin-throwers, carefree
despite punishing practices, screaming orders,
despite limbs trained to turn lethal for mobs
unable to bear the thought of two men
clinging to life, but here it's only the thock
of wooden sword against wooden sword,
the racket as they fall on each other's shields
in joy. Pugnax's heart breaks for them.
Understand, he has inflicted pain and felt pain,

but now wants to go native, move into a flat,
experiment with fashionable clothes,
dawdle at the baths, tame his nights with tea,
be spellbound by the smell of soap, find a wife.
Our boy dreams of joining the crowd,
shouting himself hoarse as some bonehead
gets knocked down and the blade pushed
though his chest, stapling him to the ground.
At intermission, he'll watch as the blood
is raked over with sand, thinking chore thoughts:
yard work, paint jobs, weekend projects.

SANTA MARIA DEL POPOLO

Join at the joint of noon, start with a slight delay,
two hold back and two go on, and what they try to say

climbs the commotion of itself, fed, pushing its way
like a pent-up head of water, so that each smack of contact, each outlay

of peal, each throatful of clout and clang is a melee
moving to the brink of racket, and when the notes spray
we lower our voices, ears to the air, the erupting ave

bone-heard. High-strung, touch-sensitive, suddenly supernumerary, fey,
racing past each other in surging deceleration, runaway

and woken through, four clappers knocked into flower, into epic play,

until our heartbeats slow, mid-swing, stalling to a sway;
slack, slaked, huge and half elsewhere, the heaven-taken grey
hanging in belfry darkness, sacks to dry till Sunday.

FLEA MARKET ECLOGUE

Pickpocket: Don't bother. Parked in your pocket,
my hand weighs less than a breeze.
Then, with a gentleness that wouldn't nose
a balloon out of turn, you're freed,
flensed, a siphoning later felt as cold-sweat
when you stop, palm on plucked part.
Wise up. You go safe only by my good grace.
Got that? Well-fed, fresh-pressed,
powerless as the air I part. Or not?

Mark: Whatever. Fact is, you looked barely ten,
a street-soiled kid. And those fingers
loosening the noose of my sister-in-law's purse?
Caught by the speed of my *own* hand.
You backed away, crybaby trying not to.
Some strolling bravo you were!
Your glare an aerosol of charged particles
that crackled and spat between us, twitching
mind hungry to filch ounces, fish jots.

DOGE'S DUNGEON

Cave art by psychotics or Tourette's syndrome blog.
Now and then a wish—big tits, vast slit, open maw—
rises heartbreakingly out of all that scrawl. Scribal eye candy
but deranged: itchy arabesques, squirming cursive.
The founding Flarfists, late into the night, hitting send.
No white space left unsmutted, stone sets up a streaming feed
of goodbyes, first thought, last thought, final tries
at slapping oblivion's slate with harm. Twelfth-century taggers
penned to the same spot, chain gang signmaking, a school of jot,
or an open-source attack on writer's block: *le mot just*
etched, x-ed, re-etched until it became the Codex Sinaiticus
of crackpot talk, ravings.com, the hive mind in cubicles
clacking away in flame wars with fate. omg. plz hlp me. i dun wnt
2 die hre—hex and hiss and ubi sunt spam scripts
of those who tried to lockpick these fume-brown walls (:-o).
Matchstick men, cornered, text-messaging their terror.

DELTA HOTEL, SAINT JOHN

What kind of boys are these? Sucker-punch boys,
headlock boys, lunch-heist boys, wedgie boys,
boys with heavy rumps, interred pecs and belts
that pay out paunches. Add one-syllable, handgripping names,
add Blackberries and the latest learned terms:
client-led cascading process, new kinds of lock-in.
In the lobby, like an airport lounge between time zones,
I spot myself: dark Tip Top suit gone to seed,
blue dress shirt, leather lace-ups, and, as he walks by,
the over-sweet, body-heat smell of cologne.
I know all about the cradle-to-grave schlep his life has become,
days when flourescent-lit is as visionary as it gets.
His love of winning, and the way winning flees
from his love for it, the three-colour business cards
he hoped would finally bring him into his own,
his wife's voice forever blinking on the hotel room phone,
the view that's nothing to e-mail home about.
I trail him into the stalls, stand shoulder-to-shoulder
as we share a pee. His good tie, knotted crisply
back in 2003. He washes his hands, stares a spell
in the mirror: bluffing himself, watching for tells.

2

LUCKY ME

Luck, for me, began at three with the hands
my father drew behind him and, between them,

traded a quarter, a candy, a stick of Trident,
whatever he could fish up from his pockets

nights when I'd surprise him in the hallway
as he stumbled in after nearly twenty-four hours

driving cab, late for dinner, and likely broke.
He'd kneel, place a finger on his lips—*shhh*—

and face flushed from the cold, coat still on,
keep his eyes on mine as he bent his arms back

in half-nelsons for an unseen game of catch.
He appeared as though under arrest, in cuffs.

This was before I learnt about the real him,
the second life he led in half-lit card rooms,

basements with two or three tables operating,
where he sat at ease among his only peers.

This was before I came across him in books,
nineteenth-century tales of titled reprobates

and debauched aristocrats—Eugene Onegin,
Will Dare, Dunsey Cass, George Somerset—

hail-fellows-well-met who never got their
shit together, and who, in their insouciance,

assumed the sweat and staleness that seemed
always to cling to my father and made him

sensationally alive. Lean, jokey, boyish,
a thirty-year-old man already on the dwindling

edge of his options, who left no deal undealt,
and who, some nights, stretched out to me

two fists, knuckles up, ready to be rapped.
I tapped one. And slowly, so slowly it was showmanship,

he spread his fingers, my prize on the palm.
I always knew where, always guessed right.

He'd shake his head at the fluke, tip a wink
at my second sight, my mind's eye, my sixth sense.

Then suddenly grim-faced, apologetic, went
to face my mother in the kitchen, my mother

who always seemed to draw the short straw,
always found herself on the wrong end of every risk,

tetchy and resentful, glum, bombshell
of her courtship, now counting out the chores,

who never read Chopin, Woolf, Plath or Rich,
never summoned *The Second Sex* as witness

to self-deceptions about the life she was lent,
this marriage that ran riot over common sense,

a still-young wife now yelling at a boy husband
who waited until he had had enough (waited,

that is, until she started to sob) and left that room
unfussed, ultimately unrepentant, hearthrob

with his umpteenth cigarette, quarter-inch stubble,
coat collar flipped up, the Great Illusionist

in full regalia. But what did I know? Those
seemed to me his finest hours. Of course

I grew up, saw the light, adjusted my sight
to the person he was—a smirking Peter Pan,

rigged on the stage-wire of his own self-love.
But the upshot is how he had me convinced

his two-fist monte was a trial of sorts, a test,
that my luck would make good on its promise,

that all I deserved would take root, bear fruit,
and I would never use up what my life would yield.

I believed it, yes. But as I learned from Chekhov,
luck's real work, at times, is shutting illusions off.

Yesterday I watched a young man kneel down
to a girl bawling in the street. He reached behind his back

—this, after years of saying my father loved me
"the only way he knew best"—and saw two treats,

one inside each palm, which he held out in fists.
Of course she was dead on, stopped crying, amazed

her choice, once again, was true and real and right.
I once had a story to tell, a sad one, about a father

and the family he never worked for, cared for,
spared much thought for; a hard-luck have-not waiting

for a huge payout that was never in the cards.
But now I think of the luck that brought you to me

and I thank a luck that flowed from yellowed fingers,
a luck that had a cigarette-smell, casual shoulders,

a luck that drained the years of the wife it touched,
left her sitting with pursed lips and crossed arms,

a luck that began at three, with a man with no luck,
who—wit of the debtor, humour of the cleaned out—

knelt before his son with two sweet, perfect bets.

TALE OF THE WEDDING RING

Who'll have me, the wedding ring cried out.
Who'll rescue me now that I'm unwanted?
I, said the earth. I'll hold you like a seam of silver,
hide you inside rock and kiss where it hurts.
Like hell, said the fire. I'll melt down your shape
and forge from it a new life: less workaday,
less fixed, more fluid, no strife. No way, said the water.
I'll wash your mind clean and you'll wake
to a cool, clear-running forgetfulness,
refreshed. Forget it, said the tree. I can play the part.
Try one of my roots for size, might fit.
Might not, said the bird. Join me in my nest:
days and nights under warm feather
and above the reach of the world, hosting
the whole of my brood. But before it could choose
the moon walked into the weeping O
of the ring's eye, wedged where it had been flung
—still pledging itself, still a trinket of its own
lost cause—and accepted it just as it was.

FILM NOIR

We were agents sifting intelligence from chatter
when static gave up the heartbeat.
                                        On screen,
a motion picture of interstellar fuzz, or fizzing

phosphorescence, shaken, full of direction.
We watched sleeper cells chase each other in dream-paced
hide and seek, dust to dust,
                                until a rorschachwise drift
came clean, until a shape, cross-examined,
snitched.
            Across from us, a suspect with a changing story.
Let's go through it one more time, we sighed.
"Hand and wrist!" he suddenly confessed.
Adrenaline pumping, we held out for the rest.

WHISTLING

And there with fingers interwoven, both hands
Pressed closely palm to palm and to his mouth
Uplifted, he, as through an instrument,
Blew mimic hootings to the silent owls,
That they might answer him.

— WORDSWORTH, "THERE WAS A BOY"

Been trying to whistle up Wordsworth's owls.
No luck. My whistling's more like whiffling.
The owls more like the shredded remains of that bird,

trapped, thrashing, on razor wire in Wyoming.

Let's bring this back to Sunday, the kitchen,
my father doodling in the margins of a crossword.
He's improvising a tune,
                              a precision-guided
piping that fills the room. I try it too; nothing
comes out clear:
                    my notes misfractioned, tin-eared.
A clean music—sweet, pure, first-personed—
needs good pressure.
                          He looks down. "Hey,
like this." His lips purse the way, when taking aim,
one eye squints for greater accuracy, and yes,

that's it—the sound I'll use to start off mine.

MORNING AFTER

The day dressed in brackish hints, morning after
we grill one-inch salmon steaks

—hiss-sputter of fat
sperm-whitening on flame. We wake downwind of dishes

unwashed, slick with marinade
and the night-long bestirring of juices

humidity now uses to goose air
wild with ripeness, morning after

not quite reek, but food-funk
butterish smelt-spores

like sun's trace on face, arms, and legs;
or milk, left out, pleasing itself.

Waking, too, to an authorless odour
quoted all around us

then suddenly cited: sweated-in staleness of leather sandals
flung in a corner, morning after

we wear nothing but garlic on our fingers,
a touch that always rubs off.

FOUR MONTHS PREGNANT

and your geezerly sofa slouch and snore bring to mind
Greek men sunning themselves on Parc Athena benches.
Over-buttoned grandpas (cardigans over shirts over tees)
who escaped the islands for years of nightshifts and sack lunches.
Sporting the crumpledness of items packed without care.
Sitting tight in warm cemetery-like weather, almost there.
Always sleepy, these last begats, chips off the old block.
Wrinkly backdrops to high noon of bird chirp and blue sky.
Droophead final acts, children married, mortgage paid.
A lifetime of waste-nothing wages, and now nothing left
but make a show of blank looks, on their mark, getting set,
until decay calls it a day and old-timer HQ closes shop,
never sure who'll punch in again, rain or shine, and nap.

LAST THOUGHTS

Life as it was: my old flat,
folding bedsheets with her.
Handing off corners,
touching briefly, stepping back.
She knew, but kept face.

By then, our bed helped too.
Nights of I-can't-take-it-any-more,
of don't-fucking-touch-me:
tucked in, smoothed out,
plumped picture-perfect

for the visitors. Newlyweds
indulging the high
thread count of happiness,
pillows side by side
in the always-been-faithful,

the always-lovemaking.
Sleepless, counting
second thoughts, I kept thinking
it couldn't have gone better.
Late for our late lunch,

you shut your umbrella,
shook it out slightly.
Brodino, you said on the phone,
and I scribbled down.
This was when the bistro

was still on St. Viateur.
It had those odd
box-like tables, shape and height
of two single beds
piled on each other.

Man, it was really falling.
I ordered a sandwich
("They add apple slices to *everything*.")
You went up to get it,
getting yours.

Chatter, plate clatter,
espresso machine hiss.
Everyone at close quarters,
shifting constantly
to let others by. We talked,

laughed mostly.
The place emptied, leaving us
in bed, each with a book,
each keeping the light on late.
I think about the clock

you picked up for a song
in Maine, insisting
it could be fixed.
Maine of the coastal glare
and brine air. Maine forever

the sharp marsh-smell
of our first summer. We hungered
for things, giddy with dreams
of our own place
and objects to fill it with.

Horseshoe-shaped
oxblood oak
appaloosaed with specks,
the busted timepiece belonged
to a local bachelor,

said the woman at the stall.
Drowsing beside you,
I think about him, I do: tossing
and turning, listening
to the ticking, his thoughts.

TO THE COUPLE IN APARTMENT 949

Stair-stompers, all-hour furniture-draggers,
hear me out: what did we do to deserve you?
Who kill time by killing peace and quiet.
Who keep your shoes on and sound like a mob.
Seriously, Jen says, looks up at the ceiling

delivering the thump of two drunks taking a tumble.
It's no laughing matter, this spigot of noise
left on and flooding our flat. We've learned
to play it by ear: bonks, konks and crashes,
bashes, rattles and clanks. Never sleeping,

you keep us awake, bipedals running roughshod.
Soon enough you'll huff and puff and plod
this house down. We've abandoned all hope.
Our walls a boom box for the pots and pans
we yearn to brain you with, knock on wood.

DEATHS OF THE SAINTS

St. Lucy, flame-proof, needed a firmly speared throat.
St. Christina's was a long job with a pair of pincers.
St. Hippolytus pitied his persecutors who faced him

blood-bespattered, breathing heavily, at wits' end
—he instructed them to bind each arm and leg to a horse
and was torn apart when all four galloped in different directions.

Those strangled, those scourged, those sawn in two.
Limbs flayed to bone. Heads that took hours to lop.
Some thrown to the lions, others drowned with rocks.

St. Simeon who begged for a stake through the heart,
said *thank you* when, heels on his chest, they thrust it deep.
And lucky St. Fergus who passed away in his sleep.

SQUASH RACKETS

For they know us by our grip and the swordsmanship
of our swing. For they are chrome lariats
always bellowing, *Here I come to save the day!*
For they love, whenever possible, the crosscourt smash
and channel our inner thug for that grunting drive.
Let us praise the harum-scarum rallies
that sound and re-sound like thank-offerings to the walls.
Let us praise the unretrievables that die in back corners.
Now a short shot, now a tight drop, and now a low
bounce caught by the lip and tipped past the T-line.
For they can throw their voice into any part of the room.
For they are patient with gimpy backhands, tinned volleys, serves skied high,
forehand boasts that are all wallop and no wattage.
For they live for deadly wraparounds,
returns knuckling down into the nick,
fast roll-outs. A pox on the slow! Let us not deal in mincing steps.
Let us lunge and stretch in the crouch-and-pounce footwork.
Oh, that moment before the quick kill, the scything slice.
For life, from their point of view, is like a camera, handheld and thrust into
    the tumult.
For they dread the moment the squeaks of our shoes move
from wolf whistle to SOS.
For they are the boo that causes a straight drive's dead run
to turn tail, double back along the rail.
For they dock the head off anything uppity, tall-poppied,
floating away on its own pretentiousness,
and thus strike a blow for authenticity.
For their ricochets crack like a nail gun snapping metal sheets into place.
For the din, getting to speed, soon turns the court cavernous and warm
with the saline, sweat-pungency of rock.

For when they mouth off they brag *belted* and *poleaxed*, *hammered* and *bashed*.
For they are always ready for what follows.
For your thumb should sit on the handle like you've dropped
the safety catch and are about to squeeze off a clip.
For a winning set is a baffled forensics that follows the bullet as it enters
and cleanly exits the whole of the imagination.
For they steal the show with boasts that whiz past the line of senses,
leaving you lightheaded with revs per thought.
For they are always punching loudness into the front wall,
bearing out your effort, marking it verbatim.
For when we miss, they go whoosh as they filter the air through their gills.
For they won't laugh at an overhead slam where you throw down the gauntlet
only to end with a bone-shaking run into the side wall.
For they know there is nowhere to go but round.
For they help the game identify itself with each noise *Walaang! Walaang!*
as if screams were being ripped from the air.
For they are quid pro quo bats,
and remind us that a soft touch
can find the shortest distance between two points.
For they let fly comebacks that flatter those bright enough to follow along.
For we lug them into a game like buckets sloshing with momentum.
For they can take a galloping rally and bring it down to heel.
For they catch the scent of direction and pull our arm after it.
For they are always spotting something up-range,
chasing the acrobounding prey until it's end-stopped by fatigue
and mid-jink they spoon that ounce of heart
—small, hot, beating in bird-panic—into our hand.
For they are cognoscenti of the counterdrop,
thought-balloons that think only one thought: sweet spot.
Or tools for what the real world lacks: a lovely, long,

levitational lob with the uncorked
reverb still ringing. You can read between the lines.
After all, the balls leave their spoor everwhere, dark c-shaped stutterings
   on whiteness,
etched echos of old volleys, and below them
us, breathless, hands on our knees, staring at the floor.

DUCKS ASLEEP ON GRASS

Knapsacks, scattered kneecaps of softness. Speckled berry-brown like soaked corks or bricks you heat to chase the chill from bed. But also: ticking bombs, brain-boxes dreaming bird barks, heartbeats like clocks set ten minutes ahead. Walk softly! Panic buttons, they are, and the smallest sound will—

VIRGINIA

No monkey business, it took all afternoon.
The tractor cut swaths I couldn't free my mind of,
and now, *mezzo del cammin*, I'm faced
with hay. What alfalfa comes to after dream days
pointing heavenward: raked and piled,
left out, low tech, to dry, sweeten to a good-looking gloss.
And before anything's lost,
just as it's taking a shine to the sunlight,
the crop's swept up, compressed,
and during a slow drive on the straightaways
rolled off with the kick of a throwing leg.
Here and there the air nicked with sneeze traces.
I'm ready to take it all to heart,
but with so much still to do
there's no excuse for simply staring.
Run ragged, the field's in pieces:
50-pound pond-green packages
bound and ready for shelving.
First editions, complete with gold leaf and slipcase,
summer stories for the cows to chew over
through the winter months.
Recto-verso invitations to renounce
everything wild that can be tied off with twine,
forked to long, wasp-filled racks
and left to stand for itself.
Nothing undone, nothing half-attended,
something to forget until on a morning of stacked mist
the wind drops everything to pick up its scent.

PIMPINELLA

Herb's death-bed sleep
at an open window.
Piled in a pan, clipped stems
join like eyelids.
Two days, and colour
keeps up appearances,
outlives the fragrance
tipped out and tapped
to empty. I think of the man
who was healed, took up his bed
and walked away.
We wait, watch the road's
production line of dust,
bereavement's run-off,
noon heat and summer light.
Fixed on degrees
of dwindling, a lush memory
replaces the desiccated,
cymbal-shake of leaves
you lift, surprised.
So discreetly did it happen
we hadn't noticed
they dried right through.

THE BUTTERFLIES I DREAMT
IN CHILDHOOD ARE HERE

Look at you, blown in from Christ knows where.
Shoulder to shoulder, silk kissing silk against the asters
in a bunting of open wing and stem, dozens strong,
seemingly self-xeroxed, an apricot spree of yellow
sprayed on green, and lopsidedly clinging as you feed,

afterward ascending on pillars of altitude, a still life.
You have a week at best, and soon the almanac
will catch up even with that good bloom and leave it
twisted shut, like a burr. There's something else
to consider in the barn-red, hay-green fact of this place:

a sparrow split open near the willows, in full sun.
But no. It's you I'd rather watch. Heavy enough
to flag a flower, you are large cups of colour set on such
small saucers, coins to keep a child's eyes closed.

3

THE STRANGEST THINGS

One has emotions about the strangest things
— W.C. WILLIAMS, KORA IN HELL

WEEPING WILLOW, PARC ANGRIGNON

More often than not, "I'm not myself" means
I wake wearing yesterday's mood,
a hand-me-down gloom
that still suits. Life, yet again, a fresh start
of dead stops. Every man for himself, and me
—boondocked in my own
corner of this backwater—
anybody's fool, running the gauntlet of self-doubt,
and always the threat
of things taking a turn for the worse.
I look myself hard in the eye:
relax, things are better
than they've ever been. And it's true.
I'm not as bad
as during that spell, when, stung to the quick,
I felt so low
lifting myself to the level of rock bottom
was a major achievement.
Yet it brings home
how sad I am, most days.
I've taken to thinking my happiness
is simply the usual sadness trimmed back
to give itself space to spill
or the respite of a new cutting taking root.
Get up, stretch, take the air, my friends tell me.
No thanks. Come what may
I prefer to sit it out, still smarting,
but something I'll deal with in my own good time,
free of mind-wandering, watch-checking.
A green thought in a green shade
put paid, or a stake in a story that never
came to much.

Wasn't always like this.
My friends and I
could slice up a day, wired.
But that's as far back as I go.
Breakdown set me straight,
without regret, or concerns about
small gestures of repair.
Greatest surprise came from
how little I could live on,
watched my hopes
shrink, unspent.
At first, I ran myself into the ground
trying to make sense of it
until, stumped,
I reappreciated solitude.
Better off alone, I go about my business.
What that means
is more than I care to say.
Mostly I keep
great conclusions at bay,
stick with small answers.
I know where I am
with that sort of thing.
Look at me when I talk to you.

Happens I get a sign,
and in my bones
know it's true.
Lately people keep their distance.
Talk stops when I turn a corner.
I fear the news
has spread to these parts:
my held-in shame
exposed for everyone to see,
quite beyond healing.
I'm the guy who waited too long,
and acted too late,
watched the ripeness of hope
tip toward rot.
The real story's more complicated than that.
It could have gone either way.
But I suppose now's as good a time
as any to say: I'm sorry.
Living on the run
hasn't been easy.
I can't sleep. The years
have plundered
strength and youth from me.
Still, I try to look sharp, smile as people stare.
I'll solve this soon enough.
I really should head back before it gets dark.

Too many lifelines,
fortune teller said.
A good sign, I thought,
and with good intentions
began my adventures, my days on the trot.
Loafer, spieler,
scene-stealer,
I intended to rise above it all
by staying on the surface,weighing nothing.
I got nowhere.
Louche and beachcomberish,
low-tide and loveless.
I helped the world
wash its hands of me.
Tired of my own inflated noise, pride gaffed
by the hook of something sharp,
bottomed-out,
upended. My choice now clear: go on
or go under.
Hope, in arrears,
fades to far details.

Learned the hard way
the folly of thinking
I could wear nothing on my sleeve
and everything
tucked up it. Fact is, others saw right through me.
Fact is, it hurt
and would not quit: a love
short on time,
striving to stay, but floating free.
Hardly a day.
Did it have to be so.
I'd never seen you quite like.
It was something that.
Heartbreak overwrites me
mid-sentence,
mid-phrase. What a fine thing you've done,
left my life
forever in little fits,
stutter-starts.

When I was told
the secret to success
was finding ways
to include more
and leave out less,
I began putting a bit aside,
penny-pinching
until the penny dropped
and I thought:
who am I kidding?
Tall tales swallowed at face value
left me with the buzz
of being briefly on top.
And now?
Phony, that's how I feel.
A poor man's arriviste.
So what would it take to make you happy?
You know full well.

Like any homebody,
I tread among the odds and ends
of daily subtractions.
What to make of a diminished thing
is anybody's guess.
I have enough
to be going on with
without needing to put on airs.
I'd suggest you put me out of mind
but know too well
how the barely noticed,
once spoken,
becomes the unwelcome detail you can't ignore.
I'm a nuisance even to myself
who once felt unexpressed,
and now wish
I could think about something else
besides how I give myself away
as I grow old,
as my insides break up and strew, laid open
to whatever turnabout
wind throws you off the trail. Many things
left to themselves
take care of themselves. Not me.
The little I have
I leave behind
to be found.
Lie low. Shed everything
for the lesson
of seeing it go. And so,
and so.

CAR ALARM, ST. VIATEUR

My wishes were met
with silly jokes,
trip-ups, ploys.
What kind of man e-mails himself dirty notes
and won't shut up about it?
The warning signs I ignored.
The stupid ways he tried to cue the mood.
He loved to come clean
with admissions of bogus trysts
he'd sweet-talk me
into forgiving.
Can you believe he actually rehearsed
these bouts of truth-telling?
Dummy runs in front of the mirror
to defib every flatlining word
for full effect.
Frankly, I'd never seen the like,
and now need a story
that can take his measure.
Like the one about the man
so nimble
he could stand a ladder straight,
climb to the top,
pull everything up after him.

Go ahead, say it.
Say what you're thinking.
How every fight
starts the same. A misjudged word,
misheard, and soon
the night's sunk to the hilt
in rage. The pillow talks, the heart-to-hearts,
gone. Now there are two sides to everything:
a flipped coin of moods—*amos* and *odi*—impossible to call.
First order of business
is to get it off our chest.
Pissed, we pull out all the stops: slam doors,
scream. Hotheaded,
hair-trigger, we mistake
a short fuse
for signs of life, husband and wife.

For years I bit my lip.
You were testy, refusing to be rushed.
I wanted nothing
but our plans for the future
to fall into place, for each day
to make a clear statement to the next,
a hope that hung fire
waiting for you to say yes.
The dead air
left me thinking
how much of your sense of the world
depended on unhappy endings.
I'm way past the halfway point
where one tells oneself whatever happened
happened for a reason.
When I play it all back
certain details elude me.
Your look, though, was one for the books.
There was nothing more to be said
and we didn't.

HAIRLINE WALL CRACK, STUDY, PARC EX FLAT

It takes me so long
to get up to speed,
I'm sometimes left asking
whether the job was worth starting. Afraid a foot set down
will be a foot put wrong,
I hem and haw,
think twice, weigh one direction
against another, ignore the can't-put-my-finger-on-it feeling
something's
come undone. Momentum, a work-in-progress.
I eye my options.
Eye them again. It takes time.
It can take all day.

Acknowledgements are due to the editors of the following magazines and anthologies where a number of these poems first appeared: *Arc*, *The New Quarterly*, *New Welsh Review* (UK), *The Fiddlehead*, *Dandelion*, *The Literary Review of Canada*, *Riddle Fence*, *Jacket* (Australia), and the *IV Lounge Night* anthology. "Death of the Saints" was commissioned by CBC Poetry Face-Off, held in Montreal in 2005. "Santa Maria Del Popolo" appeared on the Parliamentary Poet Laureate website. An earlier version of "Nine from Rome" received an Honourouble Mention at the 2006 National Magazine Awards. The poem was written during a six-month stay in the Eternal City in 2005, courtesy of le Conseil des Arts et des Lettres. "Squash Rackets" was a runner-up in *The Fiddlehead's* Ralph Gustafson Prize for Poetry in 2007 and later appeared in *The Best Canadian Poetry in English* 2008 (Tightrope). Special thanks to le Conseil des Arts et des Lettres and the Canada Council for the Arts for financial support, the Virginia Center for the Creative Arts, and the crack team at Gaspereau Press. CS

The typeface used in this book is Rialto, designed by the Venetian calligrapher Giovanni de Faccio and the Austrian typographer Lui Karner and issued by dfType in 1999. It is named for a bridge in Venice. AS

Gaspereau Press acknowledges the support of the Canada
Council for the Arts, the Nova Scotia Department of Tourism,
Culture & Heritage and the Government of Canada through the
Book Publishing Industry Development Program.

Typeset in Rialto by Andrew Steeves & printed & bound at
Gaspereau Press under the direction of Gary Dunfield.

7   6   5   4   3   2

Library & Archives Canada Cataloguing in Publication

Starnino, Carmine
This way out / Carmine Starnino.

Poems.
ISBN 978-1-55447-051-8

I. Title.
PS8587.T3282T55 2009   C811'.54   C2009-900220-5

GASPEREAU PRESS LIMITED
Gary Dunfield & Andrew Steeves ❡ Printers & Publishers
47 Church Avenue, Kentville, NS, Canada B4N 2M7
www.gaspereau.com